Amory Dwight Mayo

A Ministry of Education in the South

Amory Dwight Mayo

A Ministry of Education in the South

ISBN/EAN: 9783337004613

Printed in Europe, USA, Canada, Australia, Japan

Cover: Foto ©ninafisch / pixelio.de

More available books at **www.hansebooks.com**

A Ministry of Education

in the South.

BY

REV. A. D. MAYO,

BOSTON
PRESS OF GEO. H. ELLIS, 141 FRANKLIN STREET
1889

A MINISTRY OF EDUCATION IN THE SOUTH.

AT the beginning of the tenth year of our Ministry of Education in the Southern United States, we respond to inquiries for information in regard to the character and present condition of the work, too numerous to be answered by personal interview, correspondence, or occasional statements through the press. The sole object of this publication is to furnish reliable information concerning our ministry in the North and South, especially to serve as a fit introduction in portions of the country not yet visited. The testimonials from prominent public men and leading educators of all the Southern States are only a selection from a mass of similar material, and give a fair account of the estimation in which the Ministry is held where it is best known.

It is our intention to supplement this pamphlet by the republication of a number of addresses, delivered on different occasions, in various portions of the country, bearing on this work. The wide distribution of such publications and the constant use of the press have been among the most effective agencies of the Ministry. It is our pleasure to acknowledge, here, the great kindness of the leading Southern press, from the first, in heartily cooperating with our work during the past ten years.

In the year 1862, we accepted a call to the ministry of the Church of the Redeemer, in Cincinnati, Ohio, and remained in that city ten years, till 1872. In addition to the laborious charge of a growing church, we served as a member of the City Board of Education for eight years, during a very important period in the development of its public schools. The interest in popular education from the beginning of our professional life was intensified by the duties and opportunities of this position, which brought us into intimate acquaintance with the common-school public of the Western States. The great Civil War was at its most critical period, and Cincinnati was a favorable point for an outlook over a vast field of operations. The valley of the Ohio was swarming with refugees from the colored and poor white population of the South-west. For the first time, we became personally acquainted with this aspect of Southern life. Unable, from imperfect health, to join the ranks of the Union Army, our attention was all the more concentrated on the issue of the conflict and the long period of the rehabilitation of Southern society that would inevitably follow changes so radical through half the area of the Union. An irresistible impression forced itself upon us that, in some way, a providential "call" might come to ourself for useful service in this stage of the great revolutionary epoch. But no favorable opportunity appeared during the ten years of our residence in Cincinnati, although a journey of a few weeks, in 1868, through the South-west, and a valuable personal acquaintance in Kentucky and Missouri, gave occasion for much thought and confirmed our undefined purpose.

In the autumn of 1872, we removed to Springfield, Mass. (our native State), and, for nearly eight years, were occupied by the duties of our fifth and last position in a parish ministry extending through thirty-five years,— in Gloucester, Mass., Cleveland, Ohio, Albany, N.Y., and Cincinnati, Ohio. In Springfield, we were called again to the work of public school administration; and our acquaintance with leading educational people in the East, through constant lecturing, visitation of schools, and educational journalism, was largely extended. But the old desire to be of service in the rising educational life of the South grew with every year, and became, at last, an overpowering consideration. Our ecclesiastical connections with the Unitarian denomination of Christians were a bar to any position of influence in the great and good work of the "evangelical" churches in behalf of the freedmen, although subsequent experience has brought us into the most friendly and mutually helpful relations with all the Protestant Christian and Hebrew organizations. Besides, it was not as a teacher, or the representative of any religious or ecclesiastical body, or as a government official, that we desired to go to the Southern people. From the first, it seemed to us that there was a place, in this vast enterprise of educating the children and youth of these States, for a friendly private citizen of the United States, who, with some reputation as an educational worker, might go on "a labor of love" to all the people of the South, following the lead of Providence, and, with the exception of teaching, organizing schools, and becoming an "agent" of any kind, serving as "a man of all work" in a field so extensive and attractive.

With these earnest hopes and vague plans in mind, we visited Washington, D.C., in the winter of 1879, and presented our views to the Hon. John Eaton, United States Commissioner of Education, President R. B. Hayes and his estimable wife, and other public men interested in the educational welfare of the South. The idea at once found unexpected favor. There were no provisions for government aid to such an undertaking, save the hearty sympathy of the National Administration and the National Bureau of Education. The question, therefore, narrowed itself at once to the probability of the friendly reception of such a "Ministry of Education" by the Southern people, and its adequate financial support to the extent of from three to five thousand dollars, annually, from the North.

To the first of these questions we addressed ourself, through extended interviews with leading Southern members of Congress, especially the Senators, whose knowledge of the field was supposed to be most reliable. To our gratification, the statement of our intentions brought the heartiest response. Nobody opposed, all approved; and many of the most eminent Southern statesmen heartily welcomed it. In their opinion, the visits to the Southern States — then engaged for the first time in the establishment of the American system of free common schools for all classes — of an educational missionary, adequately endorsed, with a single eye to "building for the children," would be received in the spirit in which they were offered.

The result of these interviews was a subsequent visit to Washington in the spring of 1880. At this visit, a circular letter from the White House, signed by President Hayes and several members of his Cabinet, and, subsequently, by many of the leading educators in the country, was given us as an evidence of confidence in the plan. Numerous letters of introduction were also cheerfully furnished by the most eminent of the Southern public men, which placed us at once in communication with the people of the South. In this preliminary work, we gratefully acknowledge the co-operation of Hon. John Eaton, late United States

Commissioner of Education, whose broad patriotism and Christian philanthropy were so conspicuous in building up the National Bureau of Education. His successor, the Hon. N. H. R. Dawson, has also been helpful in the encouragement of our work.

The agent of the Peabody Educational Fund, Dr. Curry, and Dr. Haygood, of the Slater Fund, have been devoted friends of the Ministry.

We then turned to the practical side of the plan,— how to meet the considerable annual expenses of such a ministry. It was evident that, outside of entertainment and travelling expenses, at the utmost, little pecuniary assistance could be expected from the South. The eleven ex-Confederate States, which would be our special field of labor, were struggling with the prodigious work of establishing, for the first time, a system of free education for their children, in the face of such a complete financial ruin as had not been known in modern history. In this respect, our experience has been more favorable than was anticipated; for considerable sums of money, at different times, have been contributed by leading Southern citizens, while the well-known hospitality of the Southern people and the good will of the great travelling corporations have rarely failed us. But the money was to be raised at the North, and we returned to the city of Boston and our native State as the place to find it.

A contribution raised by Rev. E. E. Hale, D.D., enabled us to make our first visit to the South in the early summer of 1880. Our route included the Hampton (colored) and Tileston (white) Schools in Virginia and North Carolina and the public schools of Richmond, Va. This was followed by a month, in midsummer, at the first State Institute of white teachers ever held in Virginia, at the University of Virginia, and a corresponding visit to a similar body of colored teachers at Lynchburg; under the direction of Dr. W. H. Ruffner and Hon. William A. Newell, most eminent of the early State Superintendents of public schools in Virginia and Maryland.

The reception at these visits removed all doubt that we had chosen the right path. Returning to Massachusetts in the autumn of 1880, we accepted the position of Associate Editor of the *New England* (weekly) *Journal of Education* in Boston.

The American Unitarian Association, which has no system of denominational schools, voted an annual appropriation, as a testimonial of its deep interest in the common-school work of the South, with no limitation of activity or expectation of denominational missionary work. The American Missionary Association (Congregational) and the Freedman's Aid Society (Methodist) gave us a commission to visit their schools for colored youth in the South, and deliver courses of lectures on teaching to their pupils.

In this way, half the expenses of the early years of the mission were met ; but at no time since have the receipts from these and similar sources, even when supplemented by our own vacation labors, amounted to one-half the sum required for the successful prosecution of our work. The greater portion of the money has been collected in our brief summer and autumn vacations by application to friends of Southern education, largely in Boston, with occasional aid from a few smaller New England cities, and Brooklyn and New York. So far, the money has always come, though the yearly labor of its collection has almost become a burden. The increasing duties of the field work compelled us, in 1885, to retire from educational journalism. Yet the literary labors of the Ministry increase with every year, the press being everywhere open to our word. A large number of pamphlets bearing on the condition of the South have been issued, of which two, "Building for the Children of the South," and "Industrial Education in the South," have been published and widely circulated by the National Bureau of Education. This feature of the work has never been thoroughly developed ; and it would be easy to circulate an indefinite number of these publications, which are everywhere eagerly read by the people and often reproduced in the Southern press.

In December, 1880, we entered on the first extended tour of our Ministry of Education, visiting the most important educational centres and schools in Kentucky, Tennessee, Mississippi, Louisiana, and Texas, and, on the return, Alabama and Georgia, including all the larger institutions of learning for the colored people supported by the different denominations of Christians in the North. The information thus obtained in these colored schools was of the greatest value, and these pleasant relations continue, whenever we are in the neighborhood of this class of establishments. But our chief interest was enlisted in the new public schools of all the States visited. These visitations were always made on the invitation of the local school authorities. The schools were inspected, with frequent talks to the children, addresses to teachers, conferences with school boards and friends of education, numerous public lectures to white and colored people, frequent invitations to speak before legislative bodies, constant Sunday services in leading Christian and Hebrew churches, and perpetual conversation on educational topics. For six years, this work was carried on in connection with the duties of editorial writer of the *New England and National Journal of Education;* — a larger amount of weekly writing than the ordinary demand for the supply of a pulpit.

We were soon convinced that we had been led by a gracious Providence into a field of labor wonderfully broad, inspiring, and hopeful, the only difficulty being the ability of the worker to fill its vast possibilities. Not only the public schools, but all private seminaries, colleges, universities, State and denominational, Sunday-schools, and benevolent institutions were flung open. The Southern "latch-string was out," and a welcome never denied from within. We can recall no marked instance of discourtesy and but few cases of courteous non-acceptance of our proffered work. No Southern journal of influence has opposed, and no public or educational man of note has come across our path. This is the more gratifying since we have used the utmost freedom of speech in discussing the subject at hand, with the widest application of educational principles to social and public affairs, in constant intercourse with both the white and colored people. There has been no difference between the character of our addresses or our bearing as an educator in the Southern and Northern field of our labors. Usually, at least eight months of each year have been spent in the South, the remaining four busily occupied in the Northern States, with brief time for vacation.

Our habit has been, on going to a State not previously visited, to put ourself in communication with the educational authorities at the capital, and, following their suggestions, take up the work where it would tell most powerfully, especially on the common-school interest. We have been called in this way to all the sixteen States of this section, several of which have repeatedly been visited. It is impossible for a visitor to do profitable work of this sort, to a large extent, in the open country, from the sparseness of population and the difficulty of reaching the people.

But many of the important schools of the South are situated in the country, and, at numerous institutes and conventions and at college commencement seasons, we have been brought in contact with the rural districts. The teachers from the country have been often called to the county seats to meet us. But most of the leading centres of education in the South have been visited in the past ten years, thousands of teachers and school officials known, with a constant appearance before large bodies of the people, of both races, in week-day lectures and Sunday discourses. Strength has been given us to do twice the amount of work of any previous years, although approaching the time of life when men generally seek rest rather than extended labors. But the field grows broader with every year, whitening for the harvest; and, though laborers of all sorts and of great experience abound, yet our Ministry of Education, a labor of love for the people of the South, at home, with a constant effort to set before the Northern people the great element of hopefulness and encouragement in their Southern neighbors, opens each new year with a wider outlook enforcing a deeper sense of responsibility to God and the Republic. It is our special work as long as life and strength are given us to do it and good men and women can be found to hold up the hands, strengthen the knees, and cheer the heart of him whose constant prayer is for wisdom, power, and love to compass the glorious opportunity of a mission so unique and full of significance.

In these years we have probably delivered from two to three thousand addresses, reached many hundred thousand people through the press, visited the higher institutions of learning and the graded schools of the majority of the larger Southern towns, become acquainted with many distinguished Southern educators, and lived among the most progressive and hopeful class of the South;— the superior teachers, children, and youth, young parents, professional and public men, and good women;— the Educational Public, of whose labors and sacrifices for the past twenty-five years the people of the United States are so imperfectly informed, but on whose growing influence the future of these great commonwealths, and through them of the Republic, so largely depends. It is not for us to magnify our mission or to attempt to set forth in detail what may fairly be claimed as its legitimate results. Enough to say that the demands upon it were never so great as at present, as the testimonials here presented give ample assurance.

The result of our past ten years' Ministry of Education in the South has been a deeply seated conviction that this section must look to education in its broadest sense; — the training of the younger third of its population in mental, moral and religious, and industrial ways for a true citizenship of the Republic, for the solution of all its social and political problems, the development of its magnificent material resources, and the union of both races and all classes in an enduring bond of patriotism and consecration to American ideas. We have no faith in the gloomy prognostications of men who live only in the past, or attempt to reproduce the follies and perils of European society in this new land. *We work for the whole American people in working for the children of the South.*

At the end of a quarter of a century from our great sectional conflict, the most thoughtful observers of national affairs are seeing most clearly that it is no more a new South than a new East and West that must come forth from the issues of "the grand and awful time" in which our lot is cast. Called by Providence to work in the Southern portion of this vast seed-field of God and humanity, we rejoice at the opportunity to labor with such people as have given us their confidence, and, heaven willing, shall not abate our effort during the brief years allotted to us for service in this world.

A. D. MAYO.

TESTIMONIALS.

WASHINGTON, D.C., March 1, 1880.

REV. A. D. MAYO.

Dear Sir,— We have heard with pleasure of your intention to devote yourself to the general work of public-school education,— through the press, through personal visitation of schools, lectures to the people, teachers, and school children, and friendly consultation with local school authorities. Having, for several years past, been acquainted with your increasing labors in this field, and deeply feeling the necessity of this educational enterprise to which you now propose to consecrate your whole strength and time, we desire to express our entire confidence in your eminent fitness for this work, so fully assured by your extended acquaintance with the common-school systems of our country and your practical and acceptable labors, now continued through many years. We trust that, everywhere, your endeavors will meet the hearty acceptance and support of those seeking to promote a cause that appeals so strongly to the mind and heart of every true American citizen.

R. B. HAYES, President of United States.

WM. M. EVARTS, Secretary of State.

C. SCHURZ, Secretary of Interior

CHAS. DEVENS, Attorney-General United States.

GEO. F. HOAR, United States Senator, Massachusetts.

JOHN D. LONG,
ALEXANDER H. RICE, } Governors of Massachusetts and Members of
GEO. D. ROBINSON, } Congress.

JOHN EATON, United States Commissioner Education.

W. H. RUFFNER, State Superintendent Education for Virginia.

B. G. NORTHROP, State Superintendent Education for Connecticut.

M. A. NEWELL, State Superintendent Education for Maryland.

J. W. DICKINSON, Secretary of Board of Education for Massachusetts.

JOS. DE SHA PICKETT, State Superintendent Education for Kentucky.

O. W. HOLLINGSWORTH, State Superintendent Education for Texas.

GUSTAVUS J. ORR, State Superintendent Education for Georgia.

LEON TROUSDALE, State Superintendent Education for Tennessee.

J. H. SMITH, State Superintendent Education for Mississippi.

H. CLAY ARMSTRONG, State Superintendent Education for Alabama.

J. H. GROVES, State Superintendent Education for Delaware.

F. W. PARKER, Superintendent Schools, Quincy, Mass.

John Hancock, Superintendent Schools, Dayton, Ohio.
Andr. J. Rickoff, Superintendent Schools, Cleveland, Ohio.
Wm. O. Rogers, Superintendent Schools, New Orleans, La.
J. Ormond Wilson, Superintendent Schools, Washington, D C.
E. E. White, President State Agricultural College, Indiana.
J. L. Pickard, President State University, Iowa.
R. H. Jesse, President University of Louisiana, New Orleans.
Eben S. Stearns, Chancellor of University of Nashville and Peabody Normal School, Nashville, Tenn.
H. H. Smith, President Sam Houston Normal School, Huntsville, Texas.
Larkin Dunton, Principal Normal School, Boston, Mass.
W. E. Ward, President Ward Female College, Nashville, Tenn.
S. C. Armstrong, President Hampton Institute, Hampton, Va.
Amy M. Bradley, Principal Tileston School, Wilmington, N.C.
Ellen Hyde, Principal State Normal School, Framingham, Mass.
Thos. W. Bicknell, Editor *New England and National Journal of Education*, Boston, Mass.
Henry W. Bellows, D.D., New York City, N.Y.
Edward E. Hale, D.D., Boston, Mass.
James Freeman Clarke, D.D., Boston, Mass.
A. A. Low, Brooklyn, N.Y.

Washington, Dec. 19, 1881.

The Rev. A. D. Mayo undertakes a work in behalf of education in the South which has my most hearty commendation.

It would afford me great pleasure to know that every boy and girl in the land has the opportunity of a good free public-school education.

Chester A. Arthur, President United States.

From the National Bureau of Education.

Department of the Interior,
Bureau of Education,
Washington, Dec. 27, 1881.

The bearer, Rev. A. D. Mayo, of Massachusetts, in the midst of his ministerial labors for many years past, has found time for constant attention to educational subjects, observing carefully the condition of instruction, and speaking and writing frequently and with great effect upon educational topics. This love of the work has induced him to withdraw from church care and devote himself to the much needed revival of interest in education. His friends, recognizing the necessity of such efforts, and impressed with his fitness and success, have furnished him means. Two years ago, in response to invitations, he began to visit portions of the South. Last winter and spring he spent entirely there. The correspondence of this office gave abundant evidence of the welcome he everywhere received and of the satisfaction which his addresses and visits gave the friends of education. I shall count every institution and community fortunate that is able to secure a visit and address from him. I recommend him to the confidence and good offices of all on whom he may call.

JOHN EATON,
United States Commissioner Education.

WASHINGTON, D.C., Aug. 14, 1883.

REV. A. D. MAYO:

My dear Sir,— Your labors in behalf of education in the South have been full of interest to me. The plan of your work — going by your own direction, in the most informal way — accords with my judgment. Your love of the work and large observation and knowledge of education elsewhere, your ready and effective presentation of it in all its phases to all classes of people, and your devotion to the single subject of education, have given you great advantage. It is especially gratifying to me that you have so thoroughly won your way to the favor of the Southern people, who must take up this work of the education of their children if our nation is not to perish from off the earth. There is new encouragement to all who are in this work, that the Southern people come to hear you so gladly and in such large numbers. Your work has clearly increased in value from year to year, that of last winter being by far the most effective.

JOHN EATON,
United States Commissioner of Education.

DEPARTMENT OF THE INTERIOR,
BUREAU OF EDUCATION,

WASHINGTON, D.C., Oct. 27, 1888.

Rev. A. D. Mayo, well known for his unwearied labors in promoting and improving public schools, proposes, during the coming winter, to visit such places in the valley of Virginia as may be open to him, for the purpose of delivering free lectures on topics of interest to public-school officers and teachers. I hardly need to add that Mr. Mayo is a gentleman in education, speech, and character, and that he has been doing noble work for public schools and popular enlightenment in many parts of the South for several winters past.

N. H. R. DAWSON,
United States Commissioner of Education.

WASHINGTON, D.C., Dec. 6, 1886.

Dear Sir,— This letter will introduce to you the Rev. A. D. Mayo, of Boston, Mass., for many years an ardent friend of common schools and popular education in the South. Mr. Mayo is widely known, and is respected wherever he is known, as a gentleman of high character and culture, whose voice and pen have been devoted with effect to the agencies and methods of education and conduct. Mr. Mayo visits Alabama and your town in the interests of education; and I take great pleasure in commending him to you, feeling that your acquaintance will be pleasant and beneficial.

Very truly yours,

N. H. R. DAWSON,

United States Commissioner of Education.

From introduction to "Building for the Children of the South" and "Industrial Education in the South," published by the National Bureau of Education : —

"The educational labors of Rev. A. D. Mayo, in different parts of the country, are among those which have proved the most effective and have been most widely appreciated. His addresses on education in the South have been most beneficial in reviving the interests of education in that section, and have been called for there and wherever there is an interest in the success of the cause in that portion of the country."

JOHN EATON,

United States Commissioner of Education.

"For the past eight years, Dr. Mayo has been engaged in a Ministry of Education through all the Southern States. With no official relations, and with the sole end in view of observing educational affairs in the South, together with all forms of service and labor found to be practical in the communities visited, with the most hearty co-operation of the leading educators and public men everywhere, and the most kindly reception by teachers and pupils, his opportunities of studying the situation have probably not been surpassed.

"The great interest in the subject of the industrial education of both races, through the school systems of the South, the extent to which this form of instruction has already been carried, the means available for its further development, and the practical ways of engrafting it upon the present school life of that region, have all been the subject of careful observation and anxious inquiry, from the beginning of the Ministry of Dr. Mayo."

N. H. R. DAWSON, United States Commissioner of Education.

[*From the American Missionary Association.*]

NEW YORK, Oct. 16, 1882.

To the Teachers of the American Missionary Association Schools in the South:

Dear Friends,— The bearer, Rev. A. D. Mayo, D.D., has visited the South so frequently, and has been welcomed so heartily everywhere, that he needs no introduction from me. Yet, as he proposes to return thither this winter, we are desirous that he should be heard in our schools where he has not lectured, and that he should receive the hospitalities of our homes where he sojourns, in all cases where the accommodations and the arrangements in the home will render it convenient for him and the inmates. I need not commend him further, for he has made for himself a record which places him beyond the need of commendation.

Yours truly,

M. E. STRIEBY,

Corresponding Secretary, A.M.A.

[*From the Freedman's Aid Society of the Methodist Episcopal Church.*]

CINCINNATI, OHIO, December, 1881.

REV. A. D. MAYO:

I am suddenly called South, and hope to meet you in your travels. In the places you visit where we have schools of any importance, I should be happy to have you visit and address them. Nashville, Tenn., Atlanta, Ga., Orangeburg, S.C., Holly Springs, Miss., Greensborough, N.C., Marshall, Tex., Huntsville, Ala., New Orleans, La., might be visited in connection with your visits to these places and the schools of the A.M.A. Do all the good you can. If we cross each other's tracks, we will confer together on the matter.

R. S. RUST, Corresponding Secretary.

805 BROADWAY, NEW YORK, Oct. 31, 1883.

REV. A. D. MAYO:

My dear Sir,— On conference with Dr. Rust, we agreed to ask you to visit all our schools that come in your way, and speak three or four times to them on teaching. This letter may be an introduction to any of our schools; and, when it seems to you and the principal that more work could be advantageously done, you may do it.

Yours truly,

HENRY W. WARREN,

Bishop of the M. E. Church.

From Educational Associations, Missionary Bodies, etc.

[From Peabody Education Fund.]

UPLANDS, BROOKLINE, MASS., Aug. 2, 1889.

REV. A. D. MAYO:

My dear Sir,— I thank you for sending me your articles on Texas. I have read them with great interest, and I rejoice at such encouraging accounts of the progress of education, under the "Lone Star." Your Ministry of Education in the Southern States has often attracted, my attention. All that I have observed of it, and all that I have heard of it from Southern friends, confirms me in the impression that you are doing an excellent work, and doing it efficiently and successfully.

Believe me, dear Dr. Mayo, respectfully and truly yours,

ROBERT C. WINTHROP.

[Peabody Education Fund.]

RICHMOND, VA., Nov. 20, 1888.

Dr. A. D. Mayo for several years has given his best energies to the cause of education in the South. His addresses and writings have been prudent, wise, able, healthful, and stimulating. His demeanor as a gentleman and a scholar has commended him to the confidence and esteem of all good people. His "Ministry of Education" has been a potent factor in school work. To governors, superintendents of education, teachers, editors, and all interested in the true upbuilding of the South, I wish to commend Dr. Mayo most heartily.

J. L. M. CURRY,

General Agent of the Peabody Education Fund.

[From the Slater Educational Fund for the Education of the Colored People.]

DECATUR, GA., Aug. 13, 1889.

My dear Doctor,— I very much hope you will continue your gracious "Mission" in the South. Some things I know: one is, that you have been a blessing to our people. I believe you understand our case as no other Northern man understands it. I have perhaps had better opportunity to form a just estimate of your work than any other Southern man has had. I also "go to and fro," and I have crossed your path many times, and have heard those speak of your work who knew its great worth.

The good Lord send you among our schools again and again.

Your friend, very truly,

A. G. HAYGOOD,

Former Pres. Emory College, Ga., now Agt. Slater Fund.

[*From Society for Religious Education.*]

BOSTON, Aug. 30, 1883.

The Society for Religious Education commissions Rev. A. D. Mayo to visit the Southern States in the interests of common-school education.

This note is to introduce him to any friend of education.

EDWARD E. HALE, Chairman of Committee.

[*From the Louisiana Educational Society.*]

At a conference of this society in New Orleans, Jan. 5, 1886, the following gentlemen were present, the Hon. Louis Bush presiding: Hon. Louis Bush, Rev. I. L. Leucht, Rev. B. M. Palmer, D.D., Rev. J. K. Gutheim, Colonel William Preston Johnston, Reuben G. Bush, W. F. Halsey, R. M. Walmsley, Hon. G. A. Breaux, R. H. Browne, Professor R. H. Jesse, Hon. C. F. Buck, Hon. Ulric Bettison, Dr. Sanford E. Chaille, also the Rev. A. D. Mayo.

The subject of an Educational Visitation through the State of Louisiana, by the Rev. A. D. Mayo, under the direction of the Louisiana Educational Society, elicited prolonged discussion, participated in by nearly all present. The Rev. Dr. Palmer, Dr. Sanford E. Chaille, Rev. J. K. Gutheim, Colonel Bush and others, most heartily endorsed the Rev. A. D. Mayo as the best man that could have been secured to undertake this work.

Colonel William Preston Johnston handed in the following as expressing, in general terms, the views of this society concerning Dr. Mayo and his proposed work: —

The principal objects which the Louisiana Educational Society has set before itself, in default of means to accomplish larger results, are —

1. To arouse the public mind in Louisiana to a sense of our woful deficiencies in education and the necessity of remedying them.

2. To afford to those who may interest themselves in the matter, information as to school laws, the best modes for parish organization, the progress of ideas in education and pedagogical methods, and kindred topics.

While considerable interest has already been awakened in the State, and something has been done toward organization and the improvement of the schools, as yet this can be considered only the beginning. But the Educational Society does not propose to rest until it drives the last nail in the coffin of ignorance.

In looking around for a person free from local complications, thoroughly informed, an enthusiast in educational work, and whose character and talents would commend him to the good will and sympathy of our people, the Louisiana Educational Society had no difficulty in selecting Dr. Mayo, not only as pre-eminently fit, but as, by all odds, the best man in the United States for the work.

Dr. Mayo devoted himself some six years ago to the cause of Southern education. Though a Bostonian and a Republican, he determined to see with his own eyes the condition of things in the South before deciding for himself or informing others what ought to be done for education in the South. Since then, he has passed most of his time in travelling in this section, and in public discussion of what he has learned here.

The reports which he carried North were very different from the lying bulletins of the carpet-baggers, which had done so much to prejudice the Northern mind against us. While he showed a true picture of the nakedness of the land, the poverty, the ignorance and great discouragements of our populations, he called attention in a very pointed manner to the heroic efforts of our people to rise above these adverse circumstances and do justice in educational matters to both races. He testified to the real loyalty of our people to American ideas, their present fidelity to the Union, and to their native vigor and intelligence, in which he hopefully saw the promise of social progress and political resurrection. Dr. Mayo's exceptionally high character, political affiliations, and persuasive oratory secured him a hearing among the most intelligent people of the North which would have been accorded to no Southern man or Northern partisan politician, especially among the educators who wield a great though silent influence on the popular thought.

Dr. Mayo's words had a most powerful effect. I think it can be truly said that no one man in the North has in the last six years done more to soften asperities between the sections and to promote a feeling of brotherhood among the States than this gentleman.

The report of the committee was then adopted.

Dr. Palmer said that it is his conviction that the society was fortunate in securing the assistance of Dr. Mayo. During his previous visits he has won the confidence and esteem of the people here. He will go forth bearing their cordial and entire sympathy, indorsement, and support. Dr. Palmer said he would be exceedingly disappointed if his tour does not produce large results in the future. The State needs to be aroused on the subject of education, and the best way to arouse it is for the living voice and the living heart of a living man to stir it up. Under God's will, Dr. Mayo will do it.

Dr. Chaille, Dr. Gutheim, Dr. Leucht, Colonel Johnston, Mr. Browne, Colonel Breaux, Colonel Rogers, President Bush, Mr. Buck, and others discussed the objects of the tour, the educational situation and interests of Louisiana, and the necessity of promoting a spirit of organization for educational purposes throughout the State.

Drs. Chaille and Richardson have given Dr. Mayo a general letter of introduction to the medical profession of the State, many members of which were educated in the college in which they are professors, asking them to afford him every facility to make his trip a success.

Under the auspices of this society of which Hon. Louis Bush is president, W. O. Rogers, vice-president, Rev. I. L. Leucht, secretary, and Cartwright Eustis, Esq., treasurer, Dr. Mayo made an extended canvass of Louisiana in the winter and spring of 1886. He bore the following letters of introduction :—

New Orleans, Feb. 5, 1886.

To all Friends of Education throughout the State of Louisiana:

Permit us to introduce to you, herewith, the **Rev. A. D. Mayo**, who, under the auspices of our society, visits you in the interest of public education.

His labor in this grand enterprise is one of love and marked unselfishness, and therefore we request you to assist him in his undertaking to the best of your ability.

Dr. Mayo has the enthusiastic endorsement of every member of our society and of the philanthropic gentlemen of this community.

All favors extended to him will redound to the progress and development of our beloved State. Very respectfully,

I. L. Leuciit, Secretary.

New Orleans, Feb. 4, 1886.

To Members of the Louisiana State Medical Society and to all reputable members of the Medical Profession in Louisiana:

Gentlemen,— The Rev. Mr. Mayo, for the sake of his mission in behalf of public education and because of his own abundant personal merits, is entitled to your highest consideration, to your kindest courtesies, and to your most generous hospitality.

We specially request that all personal friends and acquaintances to whom these lines may be made known will give to them the same consideration which they would pay to a private letter of introduction.

Yours very respectfully,

Sanford E. Chaille, M.D.,
Dean of Medical Department of Tulane University.
J. G. Richardson, M.D.,
Professor of Medical Department.

At the close of this tour, Dr. Mayo delivered an address in New Orleans on "Education in Louisiana," which, with his report of his mission, was approved by the Louisiana Educational Society, and widely circulated by the leading press of the State.

Testimonials from Institutions of Learning, School Authorities, City Governments, Public Men, and other sources in the Southern States, — extending through Nine Years of the Ministry of Education.

[From Tulane University of Louisiana, under whose auspices Dr. Mayo has delivered several courses of educational lectures to the teachers, labor organizations, and the general public of the City of New Orleans.]

NEW ORLEANS, Jan. 17, 1889.

To whom it may concern,— Rev. Dr. A. D. Mayo, of Boston, has devoted eight years to the study of Education in the South, and I regard him as the best informed person of my acquaintance on this question. His study of it has been made in a broad and charitable spirit, and with an eye to practical conditions. His missionary zeal, his homely way of putting vigorous thought, his conciliatory address, his exalted yet expansive patriotism, and his most excellent common sense, have enabled him to achieve a vast deal of good.

Much work has been done by him under my own eye, and it has been of the best kind. I trust that he may long be able to continue his valuable services, which inure to the benefit of both the white and black races. I wish him God-speed in this great and good work.

Very respectfully,

WM. PRESTON JOHNSTON,
President Tulane University, New Orleans, La.

[Work in the City of Charleston, S.C.]

CITY HALL, CHARLESTON, S.C.,
OFFICE OF CLERK OF COUNCIL,
Feb. 14, 1882.

At a meeting of the City Council, held this evening, the following resolutions, offered by Alderman G. W. Dingle, were unanimously adopted: —

Whereas the Rev. Dr. Mayo is shortly expected to visit this city in the interest of Public Education, be it therefore resolved by the City Council,—

1. That they have learned with great pleasure of the intended visit of the Rev. Dr. Mayo.

2. That his Honor the Mayor be requested to invite the Rev. Dr. Mayo to be the guest of the city, during his stay.

3. That his Honor the Mayor be requested to make all necessary arrangements for the delivery of the lectures of the Rev. Dr. Mayo.

(Seal of City)   Attest: W. W. SIMONS,

Clerk of Council.

In response to this invitation, **Dr.** Mayo spent two weeks in the visitation of the educational and charitable institutions of Charleston, and was received with gratifying courtesies, public and private.

On several subsequent visits, Dr. Mayo has been "the guest of the city," and continued the work then begun. At the close of the first visit, he delivered an address, the report of which is thus introduced in the Charleston *News and Courier:* —

LIFTING UP THE NATION.—DR. MAYO'S LECTURE ON UNIVERSAL EDUCA-
TION.—A DELIGHTED AUDIENCE AT THE ACADEMY OF MUSIC LAST
NIGHT.

"The Academy of Music last night was filled with a large and appreciative audience to hear the public lecture of the Rev. A. D. Mayo, D.D., of Boston. The seats upon the stage were occupied by the Mayor of the city and the Board of Aldermen, a number of the clergymen of the city, the trustees and faculty of the College of Charleston, the faculty of the Medical College, the principals of the city schools, several members of the Charleston delegation to the General Assembly, and a number of distinguished citizens.

"Mayor Courtenay presided, and presented the lecturer as follows:—

"It is with the greatest pleasure that I introduce to you a distinguished citizen of a sister State, who is on a visit to South Carolina in the interest of universal education. For several years, his thoughtful mind has been considering the conditions of Southern education, and a year or two since he concluded that the time was propitious for arousing a general interest in this momentous subject. He has gone to this work with an earnest purpose to accomplish a great change, and his reward is assured. It will come to him in the near future, in the multiplication of schools, a higher standard of teaching, and the grateful thanks of tens of thousands who will have profited by his laborious and far-reaching efforts. I present to you Dr. Mayo of Boston.

"Without reference to notes or manuscript, Dr. Mayo proceeded to deliver one of the most entertaining and instructive public addresses that has ever been heard in Charleston."

Dr. Mayo was also requested to prepare an article for the press, giving the results of his observation of the schools of Charleston, with suggestions concerning the concentration of effort by the numerous excellent institutions of the city. This was prepared and published in the *News and Courier*, then edited by the late and greatly lamented Colonel Dawson.

On leaving the city, Dr. Mayo was presented with an engrossed document : —

The City Council to Rev. A. D. Mayo, D.D.

CITY OF CHARLESTON,
EXECUTIVE DEPARTMENT,
April 18, 1882.

Dear Sir,—I have the honor to transmit the following resolutions, unanimously adopted by the City Council, on the 11th of April, 1882.

"The Committee, appointed under resolution of Council to prepare suitable resolutions to be sent to the Rev. A. D. Mayo, D.D., expressive of the thanks of our citizens for his recent visit to our city in the interest of public education, respectfully recommend the adoption of the following resolutions:

"*Resolved,* That the City Council herewith express their sincere gratification at the recent visit of the Rev. A. D. Mayo, D.D., to our city.

"*Resolved,* That we herewith return to the Rev. A. D. Mayo, D.D., our hearty thanks for the able, eloquent, and instructive address delivered by him in the Academy of Music, and the addresses delivered by him in the several educational institutions of our city.

"*Resolved,* That we regard with high appreciation the zeal and interest manifested by the Rev. A. D. Mayo, D.D., in the cause of public education, and cherish the hope that his varied and earnest efforts in this direction may be rewarded with deserved success."

G. W. DINGLE.
A. JOHNSON.
A. B. ROSE.
(Seal of City) WM. A. COURTENAY, Mayor.
W. H. SIMONS, Clerk of Council.

At a subsequent visit, under the same invitation, Dr. Mayo gave his entire attention to the colored schools and people of the city. The following account of an interesting incident in this visit is from an address entitled, "The New Education in the New South":—

"More than twenty years ago, one of the bravest of the young commanders in the national army, Colonel Shaw, of the city of New York, fell, at the head of his brigade of colored soldiers, in a desperate assault on Fort Wagner, during the siege of Charleston. He was buried with his men, and his body was never found. After the close of the war, the families in New York and Boston, connected with the fallen soldier, built a school-house in Charleston for colored children, established the Shaw School, and for several years supported it as a private beneficence. Some five years since, the use of the building was granted to the public school authorities of the city, on condition of the support of the school as a part of the general system of instruction. Later still, the building was virtually given to the city, and all the funds of the corporation passed over for its enlargement; and now one of the public schools of Charleston bears the name of the New York colonel who died at the head of his black brigade, forcing the entrance to that beleaguered city.

"Last April, for the third time, I visited the city, the guest of its government,—this time for the sole purpose of speaking to, and advising with, the colored people. And I saw that nowhere in this country is there now a more thorough and honest purpose to give these people a fair elementary education than in the city that first threw out the flag of revolt and shot the first gun turned against the Union in '61. There are several large schools, supported from the North, which were visited. But the most interesting of all were the two great free schools, containing two thousand colored children, many of their teachers representing the old respectable white families of the city. No portion of the public school system receives more cordial and careful attention than this from the able superintendent, the patriotic and energetic Mayor, and the School Board, whose president is the former Secretary of the Treasury of the Confederate Government, Colonel Memminger.

My last visit was to the Shaw School, now a collection of several hundred children, with white and colored teachers; the principal, like the city superintendent, an officer in the Confederate army. After suitable inspection, I was invited to the great hall to listen to some exercises by the higher classes, prepared, as I understood, for their coming commencement exhibition. The first was a recitation, by a hundred of the older pupils, from Longfellow's 'Building of the Ship':—

'Sail on, O Ship of State!
Sail on, O Union, strong and great!
Humanity with all its fears,
With all its hopes of future years,
Is hanging breathless on thy fate !
.   .   .   .
Our hearts, our hopes, are all with thee,
Our hearts, our hopes, our prayers, our tears,
Our faith triumphant o'er our fears,
Are all with thee,—are all with thee !'

Then a boy, as black as night, George Washington by name, was summoned from his seat to recite a pathetic poem, "The Dying Soldier." It didn't need comment to show for what cause that soldier died; for the poem was a most touching story of peril and suffering, even unto death, for the saving of the Union. As the soldier neared his end, he called to his companions for one more of the old songs of the village Sunday-school; and the whole body of children took up the theme and sung, with a pathos only heard in the tones of the freedmen, the dying refrain. The soldier breathed his last with a prayer for his country; when the entire crowd sprang to their feet and, led by their teachers, pealed forth,—

'The star-spangled banner, O long may it wave
O'er the land of the free and the home of the brave!'

" Two weeks later, I stood at the other end of South Carolina, in the thriving town of Chester, in another colored school, supported by Northern funds, for the higher and industrial education of colored youth. Beside me was Colonel Coward, the excellent State Superintendent of Public Instruction. We stood in the halls of a great plantation house, and overlooked a broad estate on a beautiful hill-top, now owned and used for this end. That estate in 1860 was held by the largest slaveholder in northern South Carolina; and here was the official of the State bidding God-speed to the new work of uplifting to which it is conseccrated to-day."

Dr. Mayo visited South Carolina, for the first time, in the year 1882, bearing the following letters : —

U. S. SENATE CHAMBER,
WASHINGTON, Dec. 16, 1881.

HON. H. S. THOMPSON, State Supt. Education, Columbia, S.C. :

My dear Sir,— I beg to commend to you Dr. Mayo of Massachusetts, who is devoting himself to the cause of education, and any co-operation rendered his efforts in South Carolina will be gratefully appreciated by him.

Have the kindness to give him the benefit of your intimate knowledge of the educational wants of South Carolina, and show him such attention as his high character and laudable mission deserve.

Very truly yours,
M. C. BUTLER, U. S. Senator from South Carolina.

I take pleasure in concurring in the letter of Gen. Butler.
WADE HAMPTON, U. S. Senator from South Carolina.

A similar letter, originally addressed to the people of South Carolina, was indorsed, for general use in the South, by the following Senators in Congress : —

Wade Hampton, M. C. Butler, Senators from South Carolina.
Thomas F. Bayard, Eli Saulsbury, Senators from Delaware.
James B. Beck, Senator from Kentucky.
Joseph E. Brown, Alfred II. Colquitt, Senators from Georgia.

Isham G. Harris, Howell E. Johnson, Senators from Tennessee.
Augustus H. Garland, Senator from Arkansas.
L. Q. C. Lamar, James Q. George, Senators from Mississippi.
William Call, Charles E. Jones, Senators from Florida.
Randall L. Gibson, Senator from Louisiana.

STATE OF SOUTH CAROLINA,
EXECUTIVE CHAMBER,
COLUMBIA, Feb. 13, 1882.

Dr. Mayo visits this State in the interest of education. He brings with him the highest recommendations, and is commended to the courtesy and co-operation of our people.

JOHNSON HAGOOD, Governor South Carolina.

[*From Hon. Hugh S. Thompson, State Superintendent Education, Governor of South Carolina, First Agent U. S. Treasury, Member U. S. Civil Service Commission.*]

WASHINGTON, D.C., Aug. 24, 1889.

Having personal knowledge of the work of the Rev. A. D. Mayo in South Carolina, I take pleasure in bearing testimony to the great good which he has accomplished in arousing interest in popular education. His energy and his power as a public speaker have enabled him to render most valuable service to the cause in which he labors with a zeal and diligence worthy of all praise. I sincerely hope he will be able to continue his good work in behalf of education in the South.

HUGH S. THOMPSON.

[*From Hon. William A. Courtenay, Mayor of Charleston, S.C., Member of Board of Directors of Peabody Education Fund.*]

CHARLESTON, S.C., Sept. 1, 1889.

Rev. and dear Sir,— It is a gratification to know that your thought and labor are still enlisted in that great and good work of quickening the public sense in the Southern States for larger opportunities and better schools in this wide-extended and rapidly-developing area of our Union.

It is now almost a quarter of a century since the close of the war between the States; and as, against the sombre shadow which rested on the Southern States in those succeeding years, we recall the radiance of George Peabody's educational gift, with its manifold encouragement and its sweet message of "peace and good-will," so, in later years, in pleasant retrospect is your "Ministry of Education," which has unquestionably strengthened the whole South in its purpose to do its full duty in its educational work.

It has been my privilege to welcome you, officially and personally, to Charleston on several occasions; and I cheerfully testify to your good influence there and to the high appreciation in which your services are held.   I am yours truly,

WILLIAM A. COURTENAY.

OFFICE OF THE TOWN CLERK AND TREASURER,
BEAUFORT, S.C., March 9, 1882.

Whereas the Town Council of Beaufort has learned with pleasure of the proposed visit of the Rev. A. D. Mayo to our town in the interest of public education, and, whereas, it is the desire of council to encourage all workers in aid of this important instrument for the welfare of the Republic, therefore,

. Be it resolved by the Intendant and Wardens of the town of Beaufort, in council assembled, that the hospitality of the town be and is hereby extended to the Rev. A. D. Mayo, accompanied by their best wishes for the success of his undertaking while visiting the State.

And be it further resolved that the Intendant be requested to appoint a committee of members of Council and citizens, to meet the Rev. A. D. Mayo upon his arrival, and extend the kindly offices as set forth in the foregoing resolutions.

Adopted in Council this ninth day of March, A.D. 1882.

ALFRED G. THOMAS, Clerk of Council.

STATE OF ALABAMA, EXECUTIVE OFFICE,
MONTGOMERY, Jan. 18, 1887.

HON. N. H. R. DAWSON,
    Commissioner of Education, Washington, D.C.:

Dear Sir,— I have received your favor of a few days since, advising that the Rev. A. D. Mayo, D.D., anticipates visiting Alabama in the interest of education, and will await his coming with pleasure.

Yours very truly,

THOMAS SEAY, Governor.

U. S. SENATE, WASHINGTON, Dec. 1, 1880.

To MAJOR E. W. CABE, Houston, Texas:

Dear Major,— This will introduce to you Rev. A. D. Mayo, of Boston, Mass., who is on an educational tour through the South. His purposes are inspired by sympathy and friendship for our people. He comes to me recommended most highly as a gentleman of culture, whose time has for years been devoted to educational interests, and the benefits of whose experience will be valuable to us. Please show him attention, and see that he meets the reception he so well merits.

Your friend,

RICHARD COKE,

U. S. Senator, Texas.

COMMONWEALTH OF MASSACHUSETTS,
EXECUTIVE DEPARTMENT,

BOSTON, Sept. 8, 1883.

Reposing full confidence in your desire and ability to aid the cause of education, in compliance with the request of the Governor of the State of Kentucky, that a delegation consisting of a number of the ablest citizens of this Commonwealth should be appointed delegates to attend a convention to be held in Louisville, Ky., on the 19th, 20th, and 21st inst., for the purpose of advancing the cause of popular education, I, by these presents, do appoint you one of such delegates to represent, in said convention, in all due and proper proceedings, the Commonwealth of Massachusetts.

In witness whereof, I have hereunto set my hand, this eighth day of September, 1883. BENJAMIN F. BUTLER,

By His Excellency the Governor.

Witness the seal of the Commonwealth.

HENRY B. PEIRCE, Secretary of the Commonwealth.

U. S. COAST AND GEODETIC SURVEY,
NORFOLK, VA., Jan 6, 1882.

My dear Sir,—Permit me to introduce Rev. A. D. Mayo, of Boston, who visits you in the interests of a cause I know you have at heart,—that of education in the South. He is accredited by the President of the United States and the United States Commissioner of Education. I am sure you will like to aid him in his great and unselfish work.

C. O. BOUTELLE, U. S. C. and G. Survey.

From U. S. Commissioner, and State and City Superintendents of Education.

DEPARTMENT OF THE INTERIOR,
BUREAU OF EDUCATION,
WASHINGTON, Oct. 20, 1880.

Rev. A. D. Mayo has long been an ardent friend and wise promoter of popular education. Of all the able speakers now discussing this subject, he is one of the most effective in arousing public attention to its importance. He is always entertaining and instructive.

JOHN EATON, Commissioner.

The Rev. A. D. Mayo is a sincere and devoted friend of popular education, and an earnest and effective advocate of the cause he has so much at heart. He has achieved a high reputation as a lecturer on educational topics. On the platform, he is never dry or dull. His style is remarkable for its vivacity. He has the happy faculty of adapting his discourses both to teachers and popular audiences. He is an honest man, and speaks from conviction. He deserves special credit as a stalwart advocate of the most liberal provision for public education.

John D. Philbrick, Superintendent Schools, Boston, Mass. Oct. 30, 1880.

COMMONWEALTH OF VIRGINIA,
DEPARTMENT OF PUBLIC INSTRUCTION,
RICHMOND, VA., Oct. 25, 1880.

The Rev. A. D. Mayo is an exceptionally good lecturer on education. He always entertains while he instructs, and often excites enthusiasm. His special power is before a popular audience, or in giving to teachers liberal views. He stands up boldly for the New Education.

W. H. Ruffner, State Superintendent, Va.

COMMONWEALTH OF PENNSYLVANIA,
DEPARTMENT OF PUBLIC INSTRUCTION,
HARRISBURG, Oct. 20, 1880.

I have heard Dr. A. D. Mayo on the platform frequently, and consider him one of the ablest and most interesting educational lecturers in the country.

J. P. Wickersham, Superintendent Public Instruction.

STATE OF RHODE ISLAND,
OFFICE COMMISSIONER PUBLIC SCHOOLS,
PROVIDENCE, Oct. 23, 1880.

Rev. A. D. Mayo:

Dear Sir,— I am very glad to learn that your pen and voice are now both fully enlisted in the cause of education. I know of no one better calculated to do effective work with either agency. Whenever you have met and addressed our people, they have been more than pleased; and I have every reason to believe that permanent results have been secured, through your efforts, in every instance.

We shall certainly call upon you again.

With best wishes for a constantly increasing field of labor in the good cause, I am very truly yours,

Thomas B. Stockwell, Commissioner Public Schools.

OFFICE OF THE STATE BOARD OF EDUCATION,
BALTIMORE, MD., Oct. 20, 1880.

My dear Sir,— I cannot deny myself the gratification of thanking you explicitly for the series of lectures which I had the pleasure of hearing you deliver at the University of Virginia last summer, to the Teachers' Institute, then under my charge, and to the large audience of cultivated persons who gladly embraced the opportunity of being present. For appropriateness of subject, beauty of style, clearness of thought and general effectiveness, your lectures are not surpassed by any to which I have ever listened on similar themes.

Yours very truly,

M. A. NEWELL,

Superintendent Public Instruction.

STATE OF CONNECTICUT,
OFFICE OF SECRETARY OF BOARD OF EDUCATION,
STATE HOUSE, HARTFORD, Oct. 27, 1880.

Few clergymen in America have devoted so much time and thought and heart to the great questions of popular education as Dr. Mayo. He is a vigorous writer, an impressive speaker, and has that tact and quick perception that enable him to happily adapt his addresses to the practical wants of the company or locality he is called to address. His ample resources are drawn from wide and varied studies and experience. I can cordially recommend him to those who are seeking valuable and practical lecturers for Teachers' Institutes and educational gatherings, a service in which he has been long and most successfully engaged.

B. G. NORTHROP, Secretary Connecticut Board of Education.

IN THE SERVICE OF THE
COMMONWEALTH OF MASSACHUSETTS,
STATE LIBRARY AND OFFICE OF
SECRETARY OF BOARD OF EDUCATION,
STATE HOUSE, BOSTON, Dec. 13, 1880.

Rev. A. D. Mayo has been employed for the last three or four years by the Massachusetts Board of Education as a lecturer before the State Teachers' Institutes. He is considered to be an able writer and lecturer on educational subjects. I most cheerfully recommend Mr. Mayo to any who may desire the services of an able educator.

J. W. DICKINSON, Secretary of Massachusetts Board of Education.

DEPARTMENT OF EDUCATION,
AUSTIN, TEX., May 18, 1889.

REV. A. D. MAYO:

Dear Sir,— At the close of your labors in Texas, which have extended from the middle of January to the middle of May, I deem it proper to give you my impression of the value and effect of the work which you have done in this State.

You have visited all sections of the State, delivered about one hundred addresses on popular education, visited all of the State educational institutions, met and conversed with a large number of the leading men of the State, by whom public opinion on educational subjects is formed and directed.

I am deeply impressed **with** the value of the work which has been done by you in strengthening and broadening the sentiment in favor of public education in this State. The expressions which have reached me from the places which you have visited and from the institutions which you have addressed are well summarized by a remark of the superintendent of the city schools of Dallas, who says that "he feels himself a stronger man, intellectually and educationally, for the work that you have done in that city." The superintendent of another of our largest cities assures me that the attendance of the children in the colored schools of the city has been materially affected by the address delivered there to the colored people.

I am so strongly impressed with the value of your work in this State that I venture to ask that you will repeat your visit next year, if it shall be practicable for you to do so, as I feel assured that your work, next year, will be more effective than it has been this year. Your study of our educational condition will enable you to direct the discussion of educational themes more closely to the defects of our system, which are felt more and more by the friends of public education in this State with each year.

With assurances of highest respect and cordial regard, I have the honor to be,

Very truly yours,

Oscar H. Cooper,
State Superintendent Public Instruction.

Baton Rouge, La., March 11, 1884.

Dear Sir,— Permit me to introduce to you Dr. A. D. Mayo, of whose useful and benevolent work in the cause of education in New Orleans and throughout the entire South you have been kept advised through the public prints. I commend him to your well-known and generous hospitality.

With much regard, sincerely yours,

W. H. Goodale.

SERVICES IN CHURCHES AND SUNDAY-SCHOOLS, AND MORAL AND RELIGIOUS ADDRESSES.

One of the most effective features of our Ministry of Education is that portion indicated by the word — "Ministry." From the first, it has been evident to us that any largely effective mission in behalf of education in the South must deal in the most thorough and persistent way, with that fundamental character-training without which education is a house built on a shifting sand-reef assailed by a stormy sea.

The peculiar condition of Southern society emphasizes this fact. Without admitting the reckless and uncharitable impeachment of the colored population as hopelessly immoral, the most hopeful friends of this race know too well that the permanent structure of good citizenship for the seven millions of their people must be laid in the common virtues that underlie the home, industrial, social, and civil life. And, with all allowance for sectional, sectarian, partisan, and ignorant exaggeration in the North, every thoughtful Southern educator understands how much is to be done in the training of large numbers of its lower white people in the virtues of a peaceful, tolerant, and progressive civilization.

The evil of youthful vagrancy is one of the most serious perils of the South, and must be taken in hand erelong. The favorable elements of the problem are the strong tendencies to religious sentiment and church observance among all classes of the people.

With these facts in mind, we have aimed to make character-training and the most generous moral and religious development the key-note of our Ministry. The work is not a lectureship, or, in any technical sense, educational in its relation to schools; although including a great deal in the line of pedagogic discourse to teachers. The larger half of our public talk is to children of all ages, and students in every variety of educational establishment. Here is the most attractive field of labor among both races and all classes; and, without trenching on properly theo-logical or ecclesiastical ground, the burden of our instruction is in that broad region where religion and morals are the soul of all worthy living and all exalted patriotism. One of the most encouraging features of our work is the hearty sympathy with our Ministry among the clergy and most influential laity of all denominations, including the Hebrew faith. It is rarely the case that we are not invited to occupy a pulpit for a Sunday discourse; and frequently the clergy unite to give us a larger hearing.

The Sunday-school has always an open door. In this way, the Sunday often becomes the best occasion of our visit, with opportunity to reach numbers in public address who are unable to attend a week-day lecture. Every denomination of Christians, whose custom permits the invitation of clergy outside their own priesthood, has extended these courtesies. The Hebrew Synagogue and Temple are hospitable. The colored folk are always ready for another sermon, especially bearing on the duties and opportunities of their new life and the training of children. It is with great pleasure that, here, we can make this acknowledgment, in which should be included many churches in the North and the religious press of all sections. We regard our present occupation not as a giving-up of the Ministry to Education, but as a natural expansion of a parish ministry of many years into the larger opportunity of the "evangelist," or missionary in behalf of the moral, religious, mental, and industrial training of the younger third of the American people, for that American citizenship which is, to-day, the noblest distinction on earth.

THE PRESS, PUBLICATION, EDITORSHIP, AND THE RECEPTION OF THE MINISTRY BY LEADING JOURNALS OF THE COUNTRY.

At the beginning of our work, in 1880, realizing the immense influence of the press, we accepted the position of assistant editor of the *New England and National Journal of Education* (weekly), published in Boston and Chicago under the efficient management of Dr. Thomas W. Bicknell. For six years this publication, most widely read at home and abroad, offered a large opportunity of communication with the educational public. The increasing demands of our Ministry compelled a partial retirement from educational journalism at the end of the sixth year. But the call for the written word has not abated. Every new year affords new openings through the general press, which, with unprecedented generosity, has opened its columns to reports of lectures, sermons, school talks, interviews, and articles in great variety, especially, in the Northern press, setting forth our general view of life and affairs in the South. To these articles, and numerous addresses delivered and published, we are largely indebted for the hearty expression of confidence that appears in the testimonials of Southern educators and public men. The Southern press, from the first, has been a strong right hand in city and country, urging the claims of our ministry, either in • hearty approval of our views, or, with rare exception, discussing points of difference with intelligent courtesy. With some notable exceptions, the press of the North has been equally generous and appreciative of the purpose of our ministry. Several volumes of letters from the South, elaborate essays and reports of discourses, might be gathered from the leading journals and magazines of the North. The limits of this pamphlet will not permit even a selection from the notices of our work, general and local, which have abounded in the Southern press from its beginning. Of the pamphlets published and largely circulated, we mention — "Building for the Children of the South" and "Industrial Education in the South," published and widely circulated by the National Bureau of Education. Others, originally published as pamphlets and extensively copied by the newspapers, are: "The South at School," "National Aid to Education," "The City of Washington a National University," "Last Words from the South," "The South, the North, and the Nation keeping School," "The New Education in the New South," "The Normal School in America," "Governor Butler and the Schools of Massachusetts," "The Common School and Common Morality," "The Academy, Old and New," "American Brains in American Hands," "A Southern Graded School," "The Educational Situation in the South," "The Training of the Southern Teacher," "The New Version of the Children in the Wood."

OUR MINISTRY TO THE COLORED PEOPLE OF THE SOUTH.

Our first visit to a Southern school, in May, 1880, was to the celebrated Hampton Institute for colored and Indian students, established by General S. C. Armstrong, at Hampton, Va. In August of the same year, we delivered a course of lectures before the State Institute for colored teachers, at Lynchburg, Va. In January, 1881, the first visitation' of our first extended tour in the South-west was at Berea College, Kentucky.

In 1881–82, we visited all the leading schools for colored youth established by the American Missionary Association (Congregational) and the Freedman's Aid Society (Methodist) in the South, under an arrangement to deliver courses of lectures on teaching, inspect and report on the school work, and do whatever might be suggested by the government on the ground. At the same time, by personal invitation, we did the same work in the colored seminaries established by other religious bodies, private institutions, State schools, etc. In this way, at the beginning, we were able to come into the most familiar and helpful relations with one of the most important systems of schools in the Union; — a group of possibly a hundred institutions, of various grades, in the South, that are now training the superior colored teachers for that section. Educated almost exclusively in separate schools, the colored people naturally wish to have their children taught by instructors of their own race.

A few of the Southern cities still insist on placing white teachers in the colored public schools, although, as fast as these positions can be filled with suitable colored teachers, the change invariably comes. No body of young people in any country has now a nobler field for work, sacrifice, and Christian and practical service than the better class of colored teachers in the South. In the public schools, city and country, they are protected by the organization of the system against the personal, local, political, and sectarian contentions that still work so much mischief among these people. They are regarded, by parents and teachers, with a respect equal to the Christian ministry; while in education, manners, character, and general resources, they far excel the majority of the colored preachers. The young women do excellent service, and many become experts, especially in the primary departments. The competent colored teacher in a Southern community occupies a unique position,— a man or woman " of all good work," a missionary of American citizenship to the school and the people, with the best opportunity for representing them to that substantial class of the white population pledged to the education of the colored folk. To have been in constant and confidential relations with such a body for ten years, in all the Southern States and in Washington, has been an opportunity rarely enjoyed, whose importance can hardly be overestimated. Beside this, we constantly visit the public schools of the colored people, give instruction to their teachers through lectures, talk to the children and youth, and, wherever convenient, speak to general audiences. These addresses are almost invariably in their churches, in connection with religious services, and are rather of the type of the religious lecture than a technical educational address. In all this work, great attention is paid to the important subject of industrial education, in which the leading school public of the South is now deeply interested. Especially in the schools for colored youth, some of the simpler forms of industrial education should always be incorporated ; while their higher seminaries are still doing more in manual training than similar institutions for white youth. The solution of " the race question," like " the labor question " in the North, is largely involved in the progress of the educational movement, including the church, Sunday-school, temperance reformation, and all efforts at the general elevation of the masses.

Southern illiteracy, like the same thing everywhere, is far more than ignorance of letters. It means a condition compounded of ignorance, superstition, shiftlessness, vulgarity, and vice, which involves a considerable population of these sixteen American States in a sort of semi-barbarism, against which the upper region of society struggles with all the force of desperate conviction, with only partial success. That the higher civilization of the community shall lead in all affairs ; educate, direct, and, if necessary, suppress and control the lower elements ; is the commonplace of every civilized community.

The only peculiarity of the South is the temporary power of the lower element in a transition state of society. That so few disorders break out is a strong tribute to the firmness, wisdom, and forbearance of the better class of both races. The telegram that reports an "outrage," generally originating in the lower and more turbulent classes in neighborhoods away from centres of population, is flashed into every newspaper office in the land, and read at every breakfast-table; while the patient, continuous, and powerful co-operation of the better sort of people, of all classes and both races, which has already wrought such a mighty change in Southern life, and is all the time preventing disorder and educating the people in mutual understanding, forbearance, and appreciation, goes on silently, like the beneficent powers of nature, rarely noticed by the press, and almost unknown to whole classes of excellent people through wide reaches of the Union. We are able to say with truth that, to our best knowledge, our labor and constant association with the colored people has been no bar to our corresponding work in other quarters. Indeed, it has been gratifying to note the deep interest, especially of the foremost public-school people, in the educational progress of the negro, and the cheerful co-operation of school, city, and State authorities in this part of our work. As an expression of our general views on this matter, we offer a public letter, written in response to an open invitation from a leading colored citizen of Louisiana, Mr. T. T. Allain. The offer made in our letter was heartily accepted; and a great meeting of colored people, attended by the leading white citizens of the place, was held at Plaquemine, Iberville County.

[*From the New Orleans Picayune.*]

TO THE COLORED PEOPLE.

DR. MAYO TALKS TO THEM OF EDUCATION.

In response to the letter of T. T. Allain, published in Sunday's *Picayune*, concerning the education of colored teachers, Dr. Mayo writes: —

NEW ORLEANS, March 20, 1886.

MR. THEOPHILE T. ALLAIN:

Dear Sir, I read your letter with deepest interest, because it is in the line of all I have been and am still doing in the South.

You judge rightly that I have a deep interest in the education of your people; and by education I mean the entire mental, moral, and industrial training of children and youth. In my view, all classes of American youth need this; and I speak to your people, not as freedmen, but as American citizens, everywhere, urging them to push for this as their one hope of success. For thirty years in the North, before 1865, I labored to bring freedom to your people, not only for their sake, but because I was sure that the Union, and especially the South, could only survive on the basis of a true democracy in civil affairs. I never expected to see such wondrous changes as I now behold, and can hardly believe in my own identity, as I traverse the South, everywhere welcomed by the best people of "all sorts and conditions," my message of universal education always received with as great attention and respect as in any portion of the country.

In Louisiana, I have been doing for the past five years just what you suggest. My first visit to your State, five years ago, was almost entirely occupied by work on just the lines you indicate, in the colored schools and churches of New Orleans. It is significant that every lecture I have given to audiences of white people this year in Louisiana was first delivered in the schools and churches of your people in New Orleans; and they seem equally to suit my hearers in every locality. I helped ordain one of the presidents of these schools in New York, and have never slackened in my interest and labors in your behalf.

Within the past month, I have addressed half-a-dozen large and attentive audiences between New Orleans and Shreveport. In April, I may be in your parish; and any reasonable invitation within my overtaxed strength to speak to your people will be responded to. And I should say, also, that all I can do in this way is with the heartiest encouragement of the whole educational public of Louisiana, as I everywhere come in contact with it.

You seem to me to have "hit the nail on the head" in your urgent desire for the normal and industrial training of your superior young people.

The great lever to raise up any class of the American people is the common school, taught by trained teachers, who will also enforce the idea by precept and example that intelligent labor — education in the fingers — can alone rescue the working masses from all the evils that now beset them.

Ignorance and whiskey are the twin demons that scourge your people; and the common school and the temperance reform are the twin angels that will lead them out of the most fearful bondage that can afflict humanity.

These agencies, persistently worked, cannot fail, in time, to do everything that can be done for your own as for every class of our people.

I would say that at present the opportunities for training common-school teachers in Louisiana are really better for your own than for the white people. The three colleges in New Orleans are good normal schools; and, though not free, your young people can be carried through them more cheaply than the white youth at the State Normal at Natchitoches. I find in these schools graduates of our best Northern normals as teachers. If your people could aid young men and women to come to these schools, it would be a great help. As fast as possible, these schools are including industrial training. The State school you speak of in New Orleans should certainly have a strong industrial and normal department, if it has not now; and I am confident that the petition of a strong body of your representative people to the State authorities urging this development would receive attention. I am told that your teachers also attend the institutes held by the State Board. The public school in Louisiana, out of New Orleans, has been greatly hindered for all children; but there seems to me a better day coming for it.

Permit me to suggest what seems to me, after six years' observation in every Southern State, the true educational policy for your people.

1. Close up, solid, on a common school, with good teachers and as much of industrial work, especially for girls, as can be combined within it. Insist upon that everywhere. Discourage the private and sectarian school movement, which so often destroys the public schools. Urge the people to pay the poll-tax: and, when public money is exhausted, combine to keep the school going, if possible, free to all. In great numbers of localities, if your people would thus combine, they could have a good public school, instead of dispersing their means, as too often now, with general dissatisfaction.

2. Urge your young people to begin education at the bottom instead of the top. There is no reason why your young men and women should not take the higher education when they get to it; but nobody can safely neglect foundations in building for the mind. Urge the matter of a sound elementary education, with industrial elements everywhere. This will create a soil out of which the big trees will grow naturally in due time.

3. Urge your young people, while they can, to take up mechanical, operative, and general work of this sort, that they may be ready to answer the great demand in this direction that is coming from the South. The native Southern white people, I believe, as a body, will welcome the entrance of your people on this wide field of labor; and I can see no reason why workmen should be imported from Europe to do what your own superior young folks can be trained to do as well.

4. Concentration of means on definite ends is the soul of success in the upper side of life. It was probably a century before the people of

Massachusetts stood on $30,000,000, as you people, after fifteen years of free labor, stand in Louisiana to-day. The fame of Massachusetts in education and kindred departments is owing to the early habit of saving from the lower to spend on the higher side of life. Your people can do great things, now, by the same simple method; and I know of no decent class of folk, anywhere, who will not rejoice to see them do it.

Finally, I think I understand fully all the disabilities of your people in the Southern States. But I also realize that, in the providence of God, no people ever achieved so much, in three centuries out of barbarism, as your own. You have the sympathy, the prayers, and the material aid of Christendom in every worthy effort to fill an honorable place in the industrial, mental, and moral upbuilding of the South. I see no bar against your final success that you cannot remove, in the same way that every set of people in American society is compelled to succeed. All the higher elements of Southern society are with you in this effort, and will combine with you in the gradual suppression of injustice, prejudice, and obstruction in the lower regions of every community. I always feel like congratulating the superior class of your people; for I believe no class in Christendom, to-day, has before it a grander mission than to work in the spirit of the Divine Master for the uplifting of the ignorant, the poor, the lowly, and the sinful, in the glorious mission of bringing the seven millions of colored American citizens to their own providential position in American life. And, although "neither a prophet nor the son of a prophet," I venture to predict that in due time this will be done. When I go to Charleston, S.C., my friend, Mayor Courtenay, first takes me to your great free school as one of the things which this, the proudest old Southern city, shows to its visitors with honest pride. Your children and mine, I believe, will see the day when the whole Southern people will boast of their colored citizens as one of the most valuable elements in the civilization of the South and the Republic.

I would urge your people now, everywhere, to send petitions to the House of Representatives at Washington for the passage of the Blair bill for National Aid. That bill secures full justice to your people, and is supported by a large majority of the Southern Senatorial delegation. A general movement from your side of the House, in its favor, might greatly help to its passage. So far, the nation and the people of the North have contributed, within the past twenty-five years, not less than $25,000,000 for Southern education,—chiefly for the colored people. The Slater fund is the last of these gifts, and I doubt not a portion of this can be secured for some of the schools of your people in Louisiana.

Truly yours,

A. D. MAYO.

[*Testimonial from Dr. William T. Harris, Present United States Commis-sioner of Education.*]

DEPARTMENT OF THE INTERIOR,
BUREAU OF EDUCATION,
WASHINGTON, D.C., Sept. 30, 1889.

It gives me great pleasure to say that I have known Rev. A. D. Mayo for more than twenty years, as a friend of common-school education and a laborer in its cause. In all my experience, I have never known any one able to set forth the true place and the function of the common-school system in our civilization so effectually as Dr. Mayo. His lectures have been very fruitful in creating and inspiring a healthy public opinion on the subject of education, and I have called him the fittest man as "missionary at large" of education. It is my sincere hope that he may consent to continue in this field of work, and that he may be generously supported and encouraged by those who have the best interests of this country at heart.

W. T. HARRIS.

With this testimonial of the distinguished, recently appointed United States Commissioner of Education, this "little book" of explanation and illustration of our Ministry of Education comes to an end. If too long for those who from the first have understood and generously favored the work, or apparently too eulogistic in its presentation of testimonials, we can only plead the natural desire to be relieved from the perpetual demand for explanation and incessant display of letters of introduction, familiar to every one engaged in a similar work. Space alone forbids the publication, to much greater length, of newspaper notices which represent the response of communities to which the Ministry has come. It is needless to say that in this record we have purposely omitted the shadow-side, from which no man or work of any real value is exempt. It would be easy enough to fill pages with the record of difficulties met and overcome, incredulity at home, and suspicion now and then in our field of labor; the varied trials, disappointments, rebuffs, and humiliations to be faced every new year by one who depends on the liberality and, to a considerable extent, the intelligence of a voluntary support; at times, an open, violent, or contemptuous assault from sources where charity would be glad to plead misapprehension and misinformation in the assailants. Of course, all these things are familiar to every earnest and progressive worker in that central domain of universal education from which, as from the grand hall of the house, a door opens into every department of human society. We hint at this with the view of bearing testimony to the fact that the difficulties and trials of our ministry have not been chiefly in the South, but rather from the inevitable collision of our conclusions concerning this portion of the country, after long and careful observation, with theories, honestly held, but founded on partial knowledge, often magnified by political partisanship and sectarian animosity.

Nobody has been in a situation to "spy out the nakedness of the land" more effectually than ourself, in these ten years, living among the Southern people in friendly and close observation of all developments, social, industrial, religious, and political. If, at the end of this interesting experience, we can speak with growing confidence and rational hopefulness of the steady progress of all these sixteen commonwealths, and the entire section once known as the South, in all the characteristic elements of American civilization, it is because, on the ground, in sight of both the encouraging and discouraging features of the situation, the balance more decisively every year inclines to the former. No well-informed and unprejudiced observer can fail to see the present defects and perils of the Southern situation. Every State in the Union contains a resolute body of people who, often with good intentions, are none the less working with all their might against American ideas. And, unhappily, this body is too often made the "blind" behind which the forces of human selfishness, in all its hideous developments, are marshalled for the never-ending assault on the higher Christian civilization. The safety of every community consists, not in the absence of both these elements, but in the growing resolution, vitality, intelligence, and consecration of that other portion of society which is resolved "that the Republic shall receive no harm." And "the hiding-place of power" for this party of progress is always found in the reserve of righteousness and wisdom in thousands of people, hardly known or noticed, until a crisis unmasks the real forces of society, and strikes dumb and dead every revolt against the welfare of the State. Here is the standing argument for universal education in its broadest sense; — the training of the head, the hand, and the heart of every new generation according to the best methods which represent the accumulated educational experience of mankind. A generation so trained can be trusted to come to the front in any day of peril, and make impossible any serious reaction in social, religious, industrial, or civic life.

The result of all our labors and observations in this field may be summed up in this conclusion. First; the educational public of the South, in every community, is the party of progress in all the elements of a true American civilization, is everywhere becoming more powerful and influential, and, in view of its environment, not surpassed in our own or any country in the qualities which everywhere insure success. Second; the educational institutions of the South, including the common school, are as certainly in the hands of the educational public as in the North. There is no essential difference in the organization, aims, courses of study, methods of discipline and instruction, the character and devotion of teachers, between the school life of the South and the North. All apparent differences are explained by the recent establishment and experimental condition, not only of the new public, but of great numbers of the restored or newly established private and collegiate schools. The separation of the races in education seems, at present, inevitable, and, on fair investigation, appears in many ways more favorable to the mass of colored children than any system now possible to enlist general support. Third; with all the disadvantages, failures, and discouragements of the past twenty years, the new education has done more for the building up of the South, in all her permanent interests, than any, perhaps all, other influences combined. The man who says that any portion of her people has not been greatly helped in all the elements of good citizenship by the educational training it has already been able to obtain, either does not know the situation or is misled by prejudices or theories which prevent his fair estimate of the facts. We believe so much has been accomplished, already, that the conservative and patriotic public opinion of every State can be relied on in any emergency that may be precipitated in the interest of any reactionary policy or notable injustice. And never was the conviction so strong among all thoughtful Southern people that the great lines of progress are in the more complete development of the forces of universal education as to-day.

It is because we hold fast the faith that Universal Education, broadly conceived and thoroughly and persistently applied, is the saving power of the American State and the assurance of the indivisible Republic that we rejoice to labor with the noble men and women enlisted in this warfare, and, in season and out of season, summon every good citizen to his post and insist on the obligation of family, church, township, county, city, commonwealth, and Nation to co-operate in training the younger third of the American people for God's reserve in the years to come.